A Wait Worthwhile

Keys to making your waiting season a winning season

Brandi K. Epps

ISBN: 978-1-71680-290-4

Distributed by iWriteBooks Publishing, Atlanta, GA.
MyuniqueGreen.com
iWriteBooksPub.com

Table of Contents

Acknowledgements

Introduction

Chapter 1

Ponder: What is a waiting season?

Chapter 2

Prepare: Getting yourself equipped during the wait

Chapter 3

Prune: Fine Tuning

Chapter 4

Persist: Push yourself past the adversity

Chapter 5

Pray: Adopting an attitude of gratitude

Chapter 6

Press: Mesh and get in tune with God to better understand His promises

Chapter 7

Promises: Stand firm in your faith until the wait is over

Final Thoughts

A Waiting Journal

Notes

Acknowledgements

I would first like to thank my Lord and Savior, Jesus Christ, for placing this vision in my heart in the year 2017. It was at this time when waiting was the most frustrating time for me, and I used journaling as a coping mechanism to overcome that season. Lord, you pushed me way out of my comfort zone and into a place that I had to put pride aside and speak from the words you placed on my heart. You strategically had me in a season of waiting, brought me out, and placed me right back in the midst of the wait to give my audience content in its raw and uncut form. I wouldn't change a thing about this journey because it has spiritually built me up to be a testament to others along the way. I'm forever grateful to be right back where I started, because I'm able to personally use this text as a means of having a successful waiting season!

Secondly, I want to thank any, and everyone, I have EVER had a conversation with about this book, from family/extended family members and friends far and wide; to co-workers and church members down to my radio show co-hosts and bible study group.

Each of you have helped push me to complete this journey and never gave up on me in the course of the three years it took to bring this book to life.

I'd be remiss not to mention the countless efforts you all have supplied. Know that you are greatly appreciated because I could not have done it without you. You all embraced this journey with me and helped me along the way. My dreams became ones that you all helped see into fruition. Thank you for holding me accountable in your words and actions, even if you only wished me luck. Nothing was too great or too small in getting this feat underway! Thank you for the countless talks and inquiries about the book, proofreading, and sharing your own stories so that I could have an audience in mind when I wrote this! WE did it! I can't thank you enough! I dedicate this to you all and love you dearly!

Finally, to my mother, Greta L. Epps, my dad, Mark J. Harris, my brothers, Jeromy J. Epps and DeVonte' A. Morton, my sister, Brianna R. Gomez, my grandmothers, W. Pearl Epps and Dorothy Webb, and my loving daughter, Blahir Elise Pearl Sorrells, THIS IS MY DEDICATION TO YOU! Thank you for giving my life purpose! Thank you for the sacrifices you've made on my behalf and for enduring this life journey with me. You all have poured substance into me in one way or another and I could never thank you enough.

It is your steadfast love and encouragement that has pushed me to complete the first of many books to come! You guys are my inspiration now and forevermore. I love you all beyond limits!

Introduction

Waiting for anything can be a drag. Waiting for a red light to change because you're already running late for work. Waiting for someone to finish a meal when you're hungry. What about when that wait has the ability to change your life's circumstances?

Maybe at some point in your life you have found yourself waiting to get into a decent relationship or be married.

Maybe you have a marriage that is flourishing, yet you find yourself waiting for a baby after you have had several miscarriages.

You may even be waiting to get out of debt and be on your way toward financial freedom—or have been on a job for ten years and are waiting to be promoted.

Nothing seems worse than waiting, right?

But, have you ever stepped back and considered that God may be strategic with His plan to have you wait?

CS Lewis goes so far as to say this:

"I am sure that God keeps no one waiting unless He sees that it is good for him to wait."

I don't believe he made this statement just because it sounds good, but rather to demonstrate that if you are ever at a point when you have to wait, it is for a just cause. I speak for myself when I say that waiting is not my most favorite place to be. So much so that it's the very reason I am writing this book. For much of the past few years I have been in what many would call a valley, a muck, or a season of waiting for the next best thing to happen in my life. While many great things have taken rise, like job promotions, moving back home to be with family, and traveling to name a few, there has always been a part of me that is still lingering on the what-ifs of life.

I am a lot like you in that I don't understand waiting and why it is necessary, but I have begun to take Lewis' statement into context; I view waiting as God's way of saying it is good for me in this moment and will bring about good in the long run. Journey with me down the waiting road and see where doing so will lead you!

Happy Waiting!

Chapter 1: Ponder

What exactly is a waiting season?

At some point or another, we have either directly or indirectly experienced being in the waiting room of a hospital. Regardless of how severe the pain or trauma, the time spent in this area feels like forever. Having dislocated my shoulder a time or *ten*, I recall these occurrences in waiting rooms to be more traumatic than the injury itself. You arrive in excruciating pain and desperately want to be seen, only to be told to fill out paperwork and wait. The pain intensifies as you share insurance information and wait even longer. To make matters worse, x-rays have to be taken and the injured area is maneuvered in a way that makes the pain seem unbearable, all the while you are yet waiting to be seen by the doctor to have the procedure. Before you realize it, you have been waiting for an undesired amount of time, to the point that you've grown uncomfortable, uneasy, irritated and any other negative connotation that comes to mind.

You see a little light at the end of the tunnel when you finally make it to the see the doctor. However, just when you think the wait is over, the doctor proceeds to poke and prod with your injury. Though these steps are necessary to ensure proper care is given, it has, again, increased the time you have been waiting to get back to your normal state. Once the tests have been run and the IV's are connected, you sense that relief is near. You can almost feel the drift from worry and defeat to a place of sheer joy and relief of the pain you were once in. When the process is over and you're at home resting, it is then that you hone in on your process and find the necessity in each act conducted by the staff, techs, and doctors. Every step you endured was purposeful, and every act had to have taken place to ensure that the procedure was handled properly. Each step brought you closer and closer to healing and restoration of the injured area.

Would you believe me if I told you that being in seasons of waiting are comparable to this very waiting room experience?

Many of us go into waiting seasons thinking: *Am I really still here?! Does God not see that I'm struggling? Does He not know how tough this is? Can't He see that I'm doing the best I can and I'm ready to receive His blessings? Why is He making me* ***WAIT****?*

Go ahead. Admit it!

You have wondered and stressed about when God was going to come through for you, asking: *When will I meet my mate? When will I get married? When will I have a successful pregnancy that leads to a healthy baby? When can I expect a breakthrough in my career? When will life become easier for me financially?* I know your wonderings because not only have I *been* there, quite honestly, **I'M HERE RIGHT NOW FIGHTING THROUGH A SEASON OF WAITING.**

Waiting seasons seem to happen at the most inopportune times, but I have come to realize that this season serves a great purpose; one that, if used effectively, can reap a heaping of blessings onto your life. As I was writing this book, I went from waiting, to receiving a blessing, and then God stepping back in and placing me back in the waiting area. You can't even imagine the frustration of feeling as if you have "arrived," and then God speaks so clearly to you about taking a step back because He needs you to wait just a wee bit longer. Quite frankly, in this season where God has boldly stated "not right now," it is one of the most undesired and uncomfortable situations I have been in. I feel as if I'm ready right now, but for whatever reason God keeps stopping the record at the part of the song that repeats "hold on just a little while longer!"

Sure, I, like you, have planted the seed. I watered the areas in my life that needed tending to.

Roots began to sprout as I grew in Christ and in the full knowledge of myself, both in and out. My flower even blossomed beautifully as I initially came out of the waiting season.

But God had other plans.

Unbeknownst to me, that caught me completely off guard. While blooming and swaying in the breeze of a relationship, my season came to an end, like flowers dying off in the winter. God stepped in during the course of what seemed like His blessing and placed me back in the position to wait again. Can you imagine that? Have you been there too? I'm learning daily that the full bloom—or God's sacred timing to bless us with the plans He has for our lives—is going to take some time. And it's in this time that we must learn to be more strategic, more purposeful, and more prepared for *whatever* we are standing in the gap to receive.

Chapter 2: Prepare

Getting yourself equipped during the wait

Comparisons

Picture this: You've logged into your social media account for the umpteenth time today. Each time you've gotten on, so and so has come up on your screen showcasing the very thing you have been praying about. You think to yourself: "Wow, they have beautiful babies!" "Congrats on the new home!" "He finally popped the question, and they look so happy!" "Dang, she's traveling again?" All the while you are secretly becoming angry, depressed, and frustrated that these same things have not come to fruition in your life. Let me just go on the record and say that as an individual in a waiting season, you will come across many people who seem to have that which you desire. It may be that they are in a seemingly great relationship, engaged, or have married the love of their life.

Maybe they have their finances are in order, with investment properties and a savings account plentiful enough to fund a four-year college education. What about the people who have been able to have children, and you have not been fortunate enough to experience this in your own life? While you should be commending them for such a feat, our humanistic, finite minds are subject to make comparisons between ourselves and others instead. In our minds we begin to develop the attitude that "they have what I want! They have what I need! Why can't that be me? I don't understand why he/she was able to get that, and I can't!

If you know like I know, comparison is nothing more than a thief. It tends to steal the happiness of your life and suck out any energy you could possibly exert toward accomplishing your end goal. I have found it easier to compare what I am lacking to people who seem to have it all and honestly, it often makes me question my self-worth and well-being amongst the unique pieces that make me who I am.

Naturally, we tend to look to others as having more, looking better, having things we desire, etc. I would even go out on a limb and say that at some point in our lives we have all had a time where we sized ourselves up to someone else's accomplishments, showing just how easy it is to lose sight of the bigger picture of the blessings that your life is already filled with. In my experiences, I have found comparison to be present most when we are waiting for God's promises to unfold.

The world as we know it has changed so much so that validation and comparison have become the norm for many of us. Social media itself has played a huge role in the way we tend to make comparisons with what is occurring in our lives versus others' lives. It often seems as if our current relationship, marital, financial and familial statuses are always on the chopping block to being compared to someone else. I know this all too well, and am guilty of scrolling through various timelines and seeing the smiles of people in these positions thinking, "she was just going on 50 million dates last year, how did she get married?" "They already have 4 children! Do they really need anymore?" "There isn't enough passport space in the world for all the traveling he's done…he can stop now!"

It doesn't make sense, does it? Those who get ahead of us relationally, financially, or from a familial standpoint are no better than we are in our finite minds, and here they are being blessed with what we strongly desire! It makes ZERO sense! During waiting seasons, however, things will always look bleak because we are at a point in our lives where transition is taking place.

What if I put a bug in your ear and told you that this season you're in is a **direct reflection of the areas needing your personal attention** BEFORE God blesses you with it.

You want a healthy relationship/marriage? Become a solid, unbreakable individual whose confidence in, and love of self, overrides the idea of simply wanting a mate! You want your finances to be in tact? Be a good steward over what you currently have by sowing seeds and becoming disciplined in preparation for more! You want to be blessed with children? Well, that has to do with your bodily make-up, but in controllable situations, take care of your body, read the books to prepare mentally, and place yourself around children so you begin to learn what is expected of parents. Whatever the case may be, God uses this time to reveal to us those places where change needs to occur, and more importantly, ways in which we need to change for the BETTERMENT OF OURSELVES FOR THE LONG HAUL! This is where preparation comes into play.

Preparation

If, during your waiting season you have been forced to compare your life to that of someone else's, I have the remedy for you: DON'T! Rather than compare, seek to discover how you can utilize this time to prepare for the blessings that lie ahead of you.

Waiting seasons are the perfect time to get prepared for what is to come.

When you are waiting, preparation is key!

If you haven't lived under a rock, you are feeling or have felt the brunt of COVID-19. In this time, we have been in the ultimate wait, to see just what will happen in our country, states, etc. Many states took on shelter-in-place orders, causing individuals to be left with substantial amounts of time to get prepared for almost anything you can think of. If you are like me, you have probably found a new hobby, started on the workout regimen you've always wanted to have, read books, spent more time with family in your home, saved money, and the list goes on. But in all the time you've had, what have you done to prepare for your next level? This pandemic may just be God's way of getting our attention to get prepared for what He has in store for us. The idle time we are given is more than enough time to make the changes necessary for what is to come.

So, get to it, ladies and gentlemen!

I have never known for an athlete to enter a game or championship without first having prepared for it thoroughly with training. Doing so would ruin any chance that this athlete had at success because the skills needed to accomplish the task don't just develop overnight. Most athletes endure late nights, early mornings, sacrificing time spent with family, money, and more for the sake of reaching their end goal. The same can be said of anyone in a waiting season.

If you find yourself waiting for any period of time, God may just be allotting you this time to get yourself prepared for your very own championship season.

As a single, seek to understand your calling in life, your divine purpose; even go so far as to discover your true likes and dislikes, what angers you or makes you happy, as these traits will be beneficial to not only you but your mate as well.

The preparations you make now will only set you up to get the most out of your relationship and/or marriage.

As a couple waiting to have a baby, read the necessary literature, go to parks to see how parents interact with their most prized possessions, and pray for a healthy baby in advance.

For those who have struggled with infertility, seek IVF options, look into adoption agencies, or just give God time to do what only He can!

If you are someone struggling financially and are waiting, find ways you can budget better with the money you have, practice saving techniques, get with a credit repair agent to help you restore and build your credit score.

Regardless of what you do to get yourself ready, *preparation for your GIFT is key and it singlehandedly indicates to God that you are ready to receive that which He has for you.*

Our God is not one to give us anything prematurely. He will dot all I's and cross all T's prior to coming through with the blessing He has in store.

My Personal Preparation

Self-assessment

All preparation begins with looking at the man or woman in the mirror and discovering what things on the inside that may need alterations. I don't care how many relationships you've been involved in, there is always something you can learn about yourself from it. Sure, you may have experienced infidelity, but what part did you play in this act? You may have even experienced toxicity, but even still, one must look within and take responsibility in the role that they played. I remember losing one of my former relationships and pointing the blame on the guy. He involved himself with multiple women at once and left me crying day in and out because of his actions. But when I removed my emotions off the table, I came to realize these red flags were present very early on in the relationship. Therefore, it was as if I had contributed to the demise of the relationship for not simply following my intuition, gut feeling, or the Holy Spirit that lives within me.

My mother always told me that what you allow is what will continue. If you allow a person to get away with mistreating you, they will continue to do so.

If you allow someone to talk to you harsh, guess what? They will feel no remorse when you bring it to their attention later. All this is being said to say while you are single, assess the areas that you may be lacking in. What can you stand to change in your life prior to bringing someone into the picture? Where exactly do you fall short?

If your dreams and aspirations have not yet come to fruition, take a self-assessment, like I did, to determine just how prepared you are to receive whatever you are asking for.

Here are some questions I had to ask myself when I became single again:

- What have you learned about yourself and how you handle relationships with others?
- What triggers you?
- What upsets you most and how do you display anger?
- How do you effectively communicate your feelings to others?
- How do you hold yourself accountable?
- Who do you trust to hold you accountable for things you may not always see?
- Have you healed from your previous relationship?
- Have you forgiven the person who hurt you in the past?
- Have you made amends with your ex, personally or to Christ?

- Will you be ok with your life if God never chooses to bless you with a mate?

Until we as singles take responsibility for ourselves, it is not a good idea to involve others in the equation. Take care of the needs of yourself FIRST, and watch how becoming complete, healed, and aware of yourself can turn itself into a blessing for your mate in the future!

Understanding deal breakers and areas of compromise in the preparation phase as a single

Along with understanding myself, I understood that boundaries and compromises must be put in place. You wouldn't dare work hard to rebuild yourself only to allow the first beautiful or handsome face to come in and wreak havoc on what you worked so hard to establish. This is precisely why deal breakers and compromises are necessary to prepare before your mate comes along.

Deal breakers are simply those things you absolutely cannot and will not tolerate in the quest to finding a mate. They allow you to stick to your guns even when our fickle, compromising hearts want to stay. Compromises are areas you are willing to bend on for the sake of helping the relationship flourish.

As a single you may not be able to detect all that you will and won't be able to handle.

Sometimes the people who come into your life are worth sacrificing your personal preferences for and this is ok. But one has to know the difference between deal breakers and compromises and act accordingly when situations arise.

Here are a few examples:

Deal Breakers	**Compromises**
Has/wants no relationship with God	Someone who knows God is head of their life but needs your help with developing this relationship
Someone who has no dealings with their family and/or friends	Someone who has had traumatic experiences with family in the past yet is seeking to mend those ties and you have the capability of assisting in this area because of your own familial connections.
Someone who is prideful and sees no issue with it	Someone who, although has faults, admits where they have gone wrong and seeks to rectify the issue at hand.

Let's talk about where you stand in the preparation phase

First things first, don't wait until you're forced to prepare—make preparations RIGHT NOW!

Start preparing for what you desire at this very moment. While I am preparing as a single who one day desires a successful, God-fearing marriage, that may not be the season God has planned for you. Therefore, you must take some time to reflect on where God has you in your wait, and where you soon hope to be. Do not allow what you see in front of you to deter you from the plans that you know have been placed on your heart. When you understand that ANYTHING YOU ASK IN GOD'S NAME CAN AND WILL BE DONE, you will see to it that you take the necessary steps to prepare *now* versus later. Your future self will soon thank you!

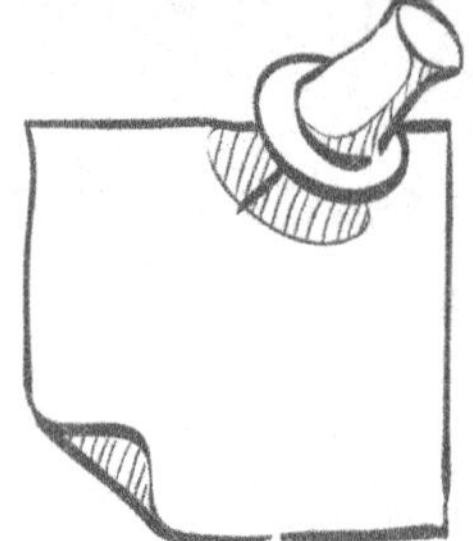

Map It Out

Ways I can prepare for parenting (if applicable)

Ways I can prepare for financial freedom (if applicable)

Ways I can prepare for a relationship/marriage (if applicable)

____

____

____

____

____

____

____

____

Ways I can prepare for ____________________ (create your own)

____

____

____

____

____

____

____

____

Chapter 3: Prune

Fine Tuning

Pruning Process

Have you ever just stared at a prune? I mean really looked at its structure and the characteristics it embodies? It is a fruit that is shriveled and dried up, lifeless even. Paint that picture in your mind. What exactly does a prune have to do with being single, infertile, lacking financial or career success? Well the fruit of course has no relevance whatsoever to any of these areas, but the act of pruning is similar to the imagery of the prune you just painted in your head. Pruning refers to ridding yourself of undesirable or unwanted qualities, conditions, or feelings. It is the process by which you are stripped of everything and anything that needs to be fine-tuned in your life. Why on Earth would anyone need pruning during a waiting season? I'm so glad you asked.

Many times, God places us in a season of waiting, not on the account of someone else, but solely based on OURSELVES! Our life experiences have caused us to develop malice, anger, bad attitudes, laziness, unhealthiness, poor spending and saving habits, overspending, lack of exercise, etc. which are of themselves undesirable when you think of the long-term effects it can have on your relationship, marriage, family, child, and finances. These are the very things that prevent one from going to the next level they are trying to reach. There is no way God can bless us in our own mess. He is a Father who will bring you to His feet BY ANY MEANS NECESSARY to get you to open your eyes to changes that need to be made in your life.

Pruning in my life

During this season of waiting, I have had to take a deep look in the mirror to understand who I was, how I came to be the way that I was or behave the way I once did. If I can be transparent for a moment: **the truth is something atrocious to view**. Our truths often reveal areas that need to change, people we need to forgive, habits we need to cease, even connections with people that need to be severed. Looking at your friends, it may very well appear that you have it all together, as if you are the most prepared of the bunch on the outside but pruning looks within.

It is an internal battle that we must fight to salvage and restructure ourselves in order to see God move in our lives.

There once was a time I was involved in a relationship that brought out some of the toughest moments in my life. Moments where I felt less than, moments where I questioned my worth, and I thought that if I could just get out of that situation, I would be ok. Getting out of the relationship was only a temporary fix, and it wasn't until I got into another relationship years later, with someone who was the complete opposite of the person in my prior relationship in a positive way, that I realized there were still stones that I hadn't yet overturned. You see, getting out of the relationship was only the initial stage of the pruning process; I had yet to heal and look within to see my own faults and how I needed some readjusting myself. I had taken the easy road, blaming another person for who I had become, and pointing fingers at this person to say that he was the sole reason for my demise.

But, I was wrong—dead wrong!

It wasn't until something triggered me in the new relationship that the realization hit home: I had only suppressed rather than pruned myself of all the bad habits I'd adopted. And what happened as a result? I lashed out and reverted back to my old ways just as soon as the trigger presented itself.

This was one of God's assessments that brought me right back to Him questioning *"what did I miss? I got rid of the old guy. Why I am still feeling like this in a new relationship if the old relationship was my problem?"* Then the light bulb went off**:** *my previous issues had less to do with someone else, and more to do with the struggles I'd yet to deal with on my own.*

Fine Tuning

As a result of looking within and being pruned, God is able to do some fine tuning. Fine tuning reminds me of a car getting a tune-up. This car may have been creaky for months, even years. Yet until it is tuned-up, it won't run or operate properly. Granted it will run, but it won't run at its best. That's like you and me. Sure, we go on about our life and never make any changes to it. A little hurt, despair, and jealousy never hurt anyone, right? A couple months without eating properly or getting annual exams surely can't hurt my body! Spending your extra money going out to eat and participating in extracurricular events is fun and exhilarating. Neglecting to save money or invest it for future expenses because you want to live your best life right now, come on, you deserve that much, right? WRONG!

In the waiting period, we have the chance of a lifetime to see errors and fix them prior to being blessed with whatever we may be waiting on.

I have heard numerous people say that whatever you don't fix in the present, will resurface in your future.

We'd be fooling ourselves to believe that the inner issues we have just magically disappear over time when they aren't addressed. That sounds a lot like the debt on our credit that people believe falls off after seven years. Why pay it if it'll just disappear anyway? Sorry, but this is simply not true of credit or bad habits we have formed over the years!

The very things we suppress and don't allow ourselves to be pruned of will nine times out of ten pop back up in our lives like a jack-in-the-box under pressure in its box. The more you are twisted, turned, poked, and prodded, the sooner your true colors will be revealed, and your problems solved. I'm so glad that God is a God who created us and knows what we need even when we don't fully comprehend what He is doing. He helps us to not only see areas of improvement, but to make the necessary changes before they wreck us completely.

Next Steps

I share all this in hopes that you take a few pointers from me when you try to run from the pruning process.

- Look within to see where changes on your part need to be made

- Before jumping into "the next best thing" take time to get rid of old habits and missteps so their likelihood of resurfacing is slim to none
- Take ownership of your faults; people and things play a part in our demise, but ultimately, we have to be willing to see the errors on our own parts and fix this accordingly
- Make amends as needed, including forgiving yourself
- Don't be afraid to start over if things don't align as you'd hoped
- Check yourself before you wreck yourself!

Whatever your next step may be, prune yourself of YOURSELF because change begins with you. No matter the role others played in your life, your happiness, future, and most importantly, your contentment**, brews first within you. Nothing and no one is responsible for this except YOU.** Take the necessary steps, prune yourself of your former self, and watch how change manifests itself almost instantly---one step, one day, one change at a time!

Chapter 4: Persist

Push yourself past the adversity

Keep on pressing on

Have you ever known that you were ready to receive a blessing that you could feel it approaching any day now? I remember when I knew (or so I thought) I was ready to get into a relationship. I cut ties with an ex that I'd let string me along for three years post-break up and I had finally met someone who liked me for me: I'm talking natural hair, stretch marks from having my daughter and right on down to my freshly washed face. I knew he was the perfect fit for me because he made me feel the most comfortable of anyone I had ever dated. Can you imagine this? Not only had he appreciated me for me, but treated my daughter like his own, sought to build a relationship with her and everything. The kicker was when he pushed me out of my area of comfort, allowing me to identify areas of insecurity or areas I could stand to grow in.

This is truly what made my love for him manifest like none other.

While all signs pointed to this being a great fit for me, do you know we still parted ways? Not because anyone cheated or didn't like the person any longer, but because things in the long run didn't add up for us. How do you come back from this? I'm talking my dream guy: tall, nice build, perfect mixture and intelligence and swag AND YET, I WAS WALKING AWAY! Why? Because our future plans didn't align. Our needs and wants were different. The way we viewed spirituality and its importance were different. Even down to the thought of expanding our family, we often agreed to disagree. While I thought about all the joy he brought to my life, I still could not look past the fact that there were things about us that collided and would not be able to withstand the storms of life when they presented themselves. So, what did I do? I walked away FULLY TRUSTING GOD AND THANKING HIM FOR HIS PROTECTION! This is equivalent to persistence, or **a firm or obstinate continuance in a course of action in spite of difficulty or opposition.**

Adversity in the waiting season is almost a given because at some point or another you will come across things, people, and situations that force you to make tough choices. As you wait, be so prepared and faith-filled that not even a stumbling block can cause you to lose sight of what you desire in the end.

If the goal is to date intentionally and with purpose, but your significant other is on a different page, **walk away with faith that God will help you persist right on through it**!

When nights get lonely and tears fall, **be persistent enough to count your blessings because things could always be worse**.

When you have encountered miscarriage after miscarriage and you want to throw your whole body away, **muster up the strength to persist through depressive states, knowing God knows best and will bless you according to <u>His will</u> for your life <u>IN DUE SEASON</u>!**

When you bounce from job to job, trying to find your way and they lay you off, **dust yourself off and try again. Opportunity is right on the other side of this opposition!**

When money is funny, and change is strange, **make allowances for yourself to get back on track one day at a time.**

Whatever the case, and whatever you have experienced is more than enough ammunition to push through! There is no way that God would bring you this far in your life for you to just give up at the first sign of trouble. We can't give the enemy that much of a foothold over us! Does he not know WHO we are and WHOSE we are?

EVERYTHING in our lives is part of the book that we call life. There is not a person, loss, disappointment, or upset that God did not foresee coming. While it may be new to you, it is never new to Him. It is a test to see if you have the wherewithal to push yourself right into God's arms and trust that his infinite power overrides your finite ability to understand it all. That push will be tough and undesirable, but you mustn't let it get you off course. *You'd be remiss not to gather all of your might and push right through it!*

Why I pushed through

Being in the situation I was in, many people would have just rolled with the punches, thinking to themselves "I'm never going to meet someone like this again." Quite frankly, you may never meet someone exactly like them. However, you must be confident and push through situations that aren't in direct alignment with your end goals. Trust that whomever God is preparing you for will assure you in all areas without an ounce of doubt. I'm not saying look out for perfection because that would be very facetious of me.

No one in this world is perfect.

But, you have to know when a situation has served its purpose and be diligent in persisting when this occurs. You have to know exactly what you can and cannot handle long term.

You must push through the wait for the inevitable to occur and stand on the ideals God places in your heart. Persistence fuels you to take a loss in stride, knowing that what is meant for you will flow and all else will fall by the wayside.

Your Persistence Steps

What is it that you're currently faced with in your waiting season?

How will you persist through this in your waiting season?

What do you need to come to grips with so that you can get closer to reaching your end goal?

____

____

____

____

____

____

____

Though your persistence will bring you to the halfway mark of a successful waiting season, be advised that it'll take just a little more artillery to get beyond the wait and all that it entails. It was in my darkest times that prayer allowed me to hold on just a tad bit longer.

Chapter 5: Pray

Adopting an attitude of gratitude

The "real" about prayer

There is no better way to transcend through waiting than by the power of prayer. But do you want to know something about prayer? We always go into it thinking we are going to tell God exactly what we want, when and how we want it, and think He's going to make it happen for us just as we've requested.

This is where we shift gears.

Prayer is NOT ABOUT US!

Not today, not tomorrow, not even in the future when we're on the other side of this waiting season, living bountifully with the blessings we are currently in waiting for. It is about God's will being done THROUGH us, and it isn't until we pray for <u>God's will over our own</u> that we begin to understand how prayer works.

Praying dangerously

I read the *YouVersion* Bible App frequently and I read a plan called Dangerous Prayers once. It mentioned that too often we pray in a way that is subtle and safe. These are those scripted prayers you've had since you were a kid such as the "Thank you for waking me up this morning" or "Please forgive me of my sins, Lord." But have you ever thought about what it means to get "dangerous" in your prayers, especially during the time you're waiting?

Dangerous, by definition, means "likely to cause problems or to have adverse consequences." So why on Earth would someone want to pray "dangerous prayers" if they have the potential to cause problems or adverse consequences? It's in these prayers that we can get real with God about how long we've been waiting, how hard it is for us to cope, how terrible it feels night after night and day after day of being stagnant. In return, He will begin to shake things up in our lives and see if we are truly "about the life" of desiring what He wills for our lives.

His will won't come to us on a paved road, that allows for smooth sailing and coasting. Nope! It just won't! Rather, it is that road that we'd least likely want to travel down. This reminds me of my tenure in Houston for 16 years and driving on the roads there.

Prayerfully they are making some changes, but if you've ever driven through Houston, you know its roads could rip the bottom from under your car (I love the city, no doubt, but the roads I can do without). I think about one road in particular, but I'll leave the name out for now. For as far down as you can see on this road, there are pot holes, twists, turns, dips and the like. As soon as you think you've dodged every dent, here comes another ready to take out all four of your tires. Those dents could be comparable to the heartbreak, heartache, miscarriages, bankruptcy, infidelity, loss of friends and family, suffering through homelessness, struggling to get pregnant, and Lord only knows what else in your life. But if you've ever traveled anywhere, you know that pot holes don't go on forever.

Off in the distance, when roads are as such, construction teams come in and begin to reconstruct the roads you once knew to be damaged. (I'm happy to update that my last visit to Houston proved they put plans in place to get those roads together! Shout out to H-Town for hearing our cries!) During construction, as previously mentioned, construction teams often transform four-lane highways into one lane, making the drive longer and drivers' patience thinner, but we never stop driving, do we? Of course not, because we ultimately want to get to our final destination.

Though construction takes forever and ten days, little by little the course you're taking gets easier and easier.

This is exactly how God works. He may have us suffer for a little, but He is never too far out of reach, looking on to see how He can use our paths to shape us into who He has called us to be. By opening your prayers up to God and asking him for that marriage, child, financial stability, career or entrepreneurship opportunity, we concurrently open ourselves up to things we have suppressed, dealt with personally, harbored for many years, and have often never shared with anyone. This makes our prayers and the wait in general that much more personable.

We have to be honest in our prayers to God and sit back and watch Him reveal to us our WHY! When we are waiting and praying, or even crying out to God, we must get serious about asking Him to reveal things to us about ourselves so that when the wait is over, we would have come out on top.

Prayer opens the floodgates of reality and shuffles in your ugly truth.

Get so serious about your prayer during this time that when these revelations surface, you thank God for them and develop a plan of attack to get through it.

Transparent Prayer

The Word of God tells us in James 5:16 NLT that "the earnest prayer of a righteous person has great power and produces wonderful results." By earnest, I mean the prayer is sincere and from the heart.

Stop right now and tell God EXACTLY what you need and desire from Him. Reach down into the pit of your body and pull out every detail, big and small, telling Him your innermost thoughts. And here's the kicker... HE CAN HANDLE ANYTHING YOU THROW HIS WAY! He knows every detail about you right down to the number of hairs on your head, so guess what this means? He already knows what's been on your mind. He just wants your dependency to fall back onto Him and off of you.

Stop and jot down your heart's desires:

Dear Lord,

I'm struggling with waiting to ______________________________ ____. I have been in this place for quite some time and honestly it feels like ____ ____. I do not know what to make of this wait, because time and time again, I have experienced____ ____. It doesn't seem like I'll ever____________________________________ ____. But I won't give up on you! In fact, I'm planning to persist in this very moment. I vow to myself to ____ ____ _________________. I know that when I am faced with adversity I tend to run, but not this time. This time, I want to____ ____. I will come out on top of this situation because I believe there is purpose on the other side. THERE HAS TO BE!

When I want to quit, help me __________________________. When I want to sulk and stay stagnant, push me to ____. Use me as a vessel at the end of this journey to sow into someone that they, too, can conquer __________________________________. I believe and receive this in the most powerful name I know, the name of Jesus!

AMEN!

I feel God moving already and I can't wait to see what your righteous prayers provide you in the end!

Chapter 6: Press

Mesh and get in tune with God to better understand His promises

Press into Jesus

Often as someone in waiting who's been in this season for some time, you have gotten accustomed to substituting your wait with idols. Maybe that idol is alcohol and you find yourself drunk from time to time trying to cope. Maybe your idol is social media and you find yourself trying to place your best representative behind a filter, being that the likes will help with self-gratification. You may have even been in relationships with girls or guys to occupy this idle time that you have. However, not even the surface level happiness that people provide is enough to sustain you.

It's in these moments that you desperately need to press into Jesus. Rather than fill the void with pointless substitutes, draw nearer to Him and His Word in this season.

It is there that you'll find people just like yourself who not only had to wait, but they waited for longer than you and I combined. Though discouraged at times, these individuals in the Bible knew that God's plan was far better than they could imagine. Now this isn't to discredit your feelings and say that you shouldn't be able to sulk and feel some type of way about having to wait–we're human so it's bound to happen–we just can't stay in that place for too long. There is hope found in God and His Word and we can trust that even pain serves as a means of purpose. Ultimately, that purpose is to get closer to Him.

Habakkuk's Wait

Waiting may seem useless, but in actuality, it has an unseen purpose rooted in God's plan for our lives. Though the wait seems like the end, it is merely a speck in God's bigger picture. I'm reminded of Habakkuk when I think of waiting. If you're unfamiliar with him, journey with me to the book of Habakkuk to gain further insight.

Habakkuk begins his journey questioning and complaining to God right off the bat about the conditions of his nation.

With violence and turmoil surrounding him, he asks "how long, O Lord, must I call for help? But you do not listen! (Habakkuk 1:2 NLT)

The Lord responds by telling him "look around at the nations; and be amazed! For I am doing something in your own day, something you wouldn't believe even if someone told you about it. (Habakkuk 1:5 NLT) Habakkuk is unsettled with this answer, so much so that he comes back firing with another complaint to the Lord about the Babylonians. He asks "O Lord my God, my Holy One, you who are eternal–surely you do not plan to wipe us out. Will you let them get away with this forever? Will they succeed forever in their heartless conquests" (Habakkuk 1: 12, 17 NLT)? You know who Habakkuk sounds like? US! Here the Lord is assuring Habakkuk of the promise He has for him, and yet he doesn't accept the Lord's words and take them at face value!

How many times have you looked at your wait, knowing that God is faithful and has come through for you many times in the past, yet you continue to question whether or not He can do what He says? At some point in our journey we lose sight of the promise and focus too heavily on the problems we see with our eyes. This is why we have to remember that God is infinite; He sees and knows so much more that what is right in front of us. In this instance of Habakkuk waiting, his focus is on the current state of his nation because it is all that he can see. However, God sees his future and suggests that he holds on just a little while longer.

The same is true for us.

Though we wait, we must hold on to God's promises and be so in tune with Him that even the idea of waiting is counted as a blessing for that which is to come.

As Habakkuk continues to question the Lord, the Lord in response pleads His Word and Truth over Habakkuk and his situation. He goes on to tell Habakkuk in Chapter 2 verse 3b "if it seems slow in coming, wait patiently, for it will surely take place. It will not be delayed" (NLT). God may be directly speaking to Habakkuk here about waiting, but there is something that we can take away from this verse:

Even if it seems like God is taking forever to fulfill his promise of marriage, children, a new position, financial gain, or whatever you're waiting for, IT WILL SURELY COME TO PASS IN HIS TIMING, WHICH IS NOT TO BE MISTAKEN AS A DELAY.

The third and final chapter in Habakkuk depicts exactly what the process of waiting will force upon you. When you have questioned God regarding the things going on around you and He has spoken and told you exactly what to do, rather than stressing about the outcome remember this: don't let what you physically see distract you from what God has said.

If He said it, He will do just that AND some, just as He did with David and the Philistine.

David boldly stated to Saul in 1 Samuel 17:37 (NLT) "The LORD who rescued me from the claws of the lion and the bear will rescue me from this Philistine!"

Believe that if the Lord has delivered and brought you through a situation or waiting season before now, He will surely do it again; as a matter of fact, I'M READY TO SEE HOW HE WILL DO IT AGAIN!

We find Habakkuk in chapter three in total surrender to his wait. Because he understands that God is in control of the outcome and his life is meshed with God's, he takes solace in his wait, giving credit to God in advance for the light at the end of the tunnel. Habakkuk, holding on to the promises God gave him in the first two chapters, shares that "even though the fig trees have no blossoms, and there are no grapes on the vines; even though the olive crop fails, and the fields lie empty and barren; even though the flocks die in the fields, and the cattle barns are empty, yet I will rejoice in the LORD! I will be joyful in the God of my salvation! The Sovereign LORD is my strength! He makes me as surefooted as a deer, able to tread upon the heights." (Habakkuk 3:17-19 NLT)

Maybe you're like Habakkuk, wondering when God will come through on His Word, providing the promise and purpose of your wait. Be obedient enough to trust the process and begin thanking God in advance for the miracles that are on the way for you! Begin to affirm yourself and your circumstances!

Even though I have been single for 4 years, YET I will still trust God for a healthy and prosperous marriage IN HIS TIMING!

Even though I have miscarried 3 babies and the doctors have told me I will never have children, YET I will trust God to bless me with a viable pregnancy and child IN HIS TIMING!

Though I don't have much money right now, I am YET trusting God to bless my finances and allow my cup to soon run over IN HIS TIMING!

Though the job market is scarce, and nothing has become available in my field, I am YET trusting God to bless me with a career where I can showcase my God-given talents IN HIS TIMING!

God CAN do it and He WILL do it when we align and press our lives with His. Pressing into Him assures and affirms the promises He has provided in His Word. Heather Jackson quotes Amy Groeschel this way: "we must trust that God will provide when it is His will and in His timing. Until then we must remain joyful, free from anger and jealousy, trusting that our Lord is in control."

You are so close to seeing your dreams come to fruition. Don't give up now! GOD HAS NOT FORGOTTEN YOU!

Chapter 7: Promises

Stand firm in your faith until the wait is over

Ladies and gents, by this point, I hope you have grown to understand the necessity in waiting. By this, I mean you have found or are finding opportunities that will propel you toward whatever and whomever it is you are waiting for.

Let's remind ourselves of HOW we are to wait:

Understand what it means to be in a waiting season **(Ponder)**

Prepare, position, and get yourself equipped for the things you are praying for **(Prepare)**

Get rid of anything within you that may be holding you back from what you are seeking from God **(Prune)**

Push past the adversity as it comes your way during the wait **(Persist)**

Speak boldly and honestly to God throughout the process of waiting **(Pray)**

Mesh your life with God's and be in tune with His Word **(Press)**

Finally, the time has come to put some action behind your faith, taking it to greater heights by daily walking out God's promises for your life. You can do this by having God's promises accessible and ready for your journey through waiting. The thing that helps me most during this waiting season is speaking life over myself and my circumstances.

It *is* hard. It gets *harder*. The only true way to survive a waiting season is to stand on what God's Word says and believe it in your heart. Walk it out daily in your actions, responses to your circumstances, and even in your reactions to the lengthy process of waiting as a whole.

Promises

Here are some key scriptures that have helped me along my journey! I hope they will serve this same purpose for you! The scriptures listed here are taken from the *New Living Translation*, unless otherwise noted.

1 John 5:14-15

And we are confident that he hears us whenever we ask for anything that pleases him. [15] And since we know he hears us when we make our requests, we also know that he will give us what we ask for.

Ephesians 3:20

Now all glory to God, who is able, through his mighty power at work within us, to accomplish infinitely more than we might ask or think.

Romans 8:28

And we know that God causes everything to work together for the good of those who love God and are called according to his purpose for them.

Romans 8:37

No, despite all these things, overwhelming victory is ours through Christ, who loved us.

1 Peter 5:7

Give all your worries and cares to God, for he cares about you.

Matthew 6:25-33

25 "That is why I tell you not to worry about everyday life—whether you have enough food and drink, or enough clothes to wear. Isn't life more than food, and your body more than clothing?

[26] Look at the birds. They don't plant or harvest or store food in barns, for your heavenly Father feeds them. And aren't you far more valuable to him than they are? [27] Can all your worries add a single moment to your life?

[28] "And why worry about your clothing? Look at the lilies of the field and how they grow. They don't work or make their clothing, [29] yet Solomon in all his glory was not dressed as beautifully as they are. [30] And if God cares so wonderfully for wildflowers that are here today and thrown into the fire tomorrow, he will certainly care for you. Why do you have so little faith?

[31] "So don't worry about these things, saying, 'What will we eat? What will we drink? What will we wear?' [32] These things dominate the thoughts of unbelievers, but your heavenly Father already knows all your needs. [33] Seek the Kingdom of God[a] above all else, and live righteously, and he will give you everything you need.

Scriptures for you to stand firm on directly related to waiting

Psalm 27:14

Wait patiently for the LORD. Be brave and courageous. Yes, wait patiently for the LORD.

Psalm 5:3

Listen to my voice in the morning, LORD. Each morning I bring my requests to you and wait expectantly.

Psalm 37:7

Be still in the presence of the LORD AND wait patiently for him to act. Don't worry about evil people who prosper or fret about their wicked schemes.

Psalm 40:1

For the choir director: A psalm of David.

I waited patiently for the LORD to help me, and he turned to me and heard my cry.

Psalm 62:5

Let all that I am wait quietly before God, for my hope is in him.

Isaiah 30:18

Blessings for the LORD's People

So the LORD must wait for you to come to him so he can show you his love and compassion. For the LORD is a faithful God. Blessed are those who wait for his help.

Lamentations 3:26

So it is good to wait quietly for salvation from the LORD.

Daniel 12:12

And blessed are those who wait and remain until the end of the 1,335 days!

Micah 7:7

As for me, I look to the LORD for help. I wait confidently for God to save me, and my God will certainly hear me.

Habakkuk 2:3

This vision is for a future time. It describes the end, and it will be fulfilled. If it seems slow in coming, wait patiently, for it will surely take place. It will not be delayed.

Romans 8:25

But if we look forward to something we don't yet have, we must wait patiently and confidently.

Romans 15:4

Such things were written in the Scriptures long ago to teach us. And the Scriptures give us hope and encouragement as we wait patiently for God's promises to be fulfilled.

Hebrews 6:15

Then Abraham waited patiently, and he received what God had promised.

2 Peter 3:14

And so, dear friends, while you are waiting for these things to happen, make every effort to be found living peaceful lives that are pure and blameless in his sight.

Isaiah 40:31

But those who trust in the LORD will find new strength. They will soar high on wings like eagles. They will run and not grow weary. They will walk and not faint.

If God included various promises and scriptures about waiting, surely, we can agree that He not only anticipated that we would wait at some point in our lives, but also that He would have the remedy for our wait. Take your wait in stride; God KNOWS far more than we can even fathom. He knows why we are waiting; He knows how long we will wait; and most importantly, He knows how integral a PURPOSEFUL wait can be for our lives.

Make no mistake that this wait that you're experiencing is NECESSARY! Some things in our lives need changing. Some actions of ours need altering. Some characteristics we've developed need to be rewired. Some people and idols need to be severed indefinitely.

Continue to hang tight during this wait, and if nothing more, WAIT WITH EXPECTANCY!

Verbally say that God is working on your behalf. Be hopeful.

Believe your answer from God will be here soon. The promises and purpose for your life will be revealed in a matter of time.

Eagerly wait for God and watch how He is going to blow your minds. I know it, I feel it, and you should too!

Continue waiting well—that blessing is closer to you than you think!

Final Thoughts

The words I poured into this book reflect my own waiting season, both past and present, and what I came to learn as a result. They are in no way the end all be all. However, if you find yourself waiting and wondering why you have been placed here time and time again, know that God is attempting to get your attention onto Him or toward some personal development within you that is lacking. Matthew 6:33 (NLT) tells us to seek FIRST His Kingdom and His righteousness, and all these things will be given to you as well. It could very well be that God is waiting on YOU to FIRST come to/seek Him and second, to get yourself together. Use this wait wisely; you never know what will happen as a result! God bless each of you and I hope that something was said or done to help you win in this waiting season!

Waiting patiently alongside you,

Waiting Journal

for

____

Utilize this space to journal every care, worry, frustration, and anxious thought about your waiting season. Take time daily/weekly to reflect on where you are, what progress or regression you've made, and where God is taking you in the process. The more you take time to prepare, prune, persist, pray, press and stand on His promises, the closer you are to WINNING in this area of your life!

Think of it this way: **Your wait may very well be the book that someone else needs to read!**

– Brandi K. Epps

Date: ______________

A waiting season is **NOT** a wasted season. -Anonymous

Date: ______________

Date: ___________

Relish in your trials, for they soon become living testimonies for others! – Brandi K. Epps

Date: ____________

Date:

God's will. Nothing more. Nothing less. Nothing else.

Date: ___________

Date: ___________

God uses our trials for the sake of helping others transform somewhere down the line. – Brandi K. Epps

Date:

Date: ____________

God knew it would come to this. It's OK. He has a plan!

Date: ____________

Date:

You've got to accept what's not for you (in this particular season) the same way you accept what is (after you've arrived).

–Brandi K. Epps

Date: ______________

Date:

Don't let what you **see** cause you to doubt what God **said**.

Date: ______________

Date: ____________

The coolest thing about God is that even a "no" from Him has goodness written all over it.

Date: ______________

Date:

Never measure your success or worth by using another man's ruler. You'll always come up short. –Cornelius Lindsey

Date:

Date: ______________

When you understand time and season, you envy NO ONE!

Date:

Date:

The best is yet to come!

Date: ____________

Date: ____________

It's hard to wait when you feel you deserve it now, but be patient so that when you get it, it's yours to keep.

Date: ____________

Date: ______________

God is **faithful** to bring **good** from even our **hardest** of times.
-Tony Evans

Date:

Date:

God's delays are often tied to our development.

Date: ___________

Date:

Being easy and comfortable doesn't change you nearly as much as the sacrifice; butterflies are the perfect example. – Brandi K. Epps

NOTES—by chapter

Intro

Jackson, Heather. (n.d.) Brave: Experiencing God in the waiting. Retrieved from https://www.bible.com/en/reading-plans/12328 (C. S. Lewis quote)

Chapter 5

Groeschel, Craig. (2020). Dangerous prayers. Retrieved from https://www.bible.com/en/reading-plans/18063

Lexico. (2020). Dangerous definition. Retrieved from https://www.lexico.com/en/definition/dangerous

James 5:16 NLT. Retrieved from https://www.bible.com/116/jas.5.16.nlt

Chapter 6

Habakkuk 1:2 NLT. Retrieved from https://www.bible.com/116/hab.1.2.nlt

Habakkuk 1:5 NLT. Retrieved from https://www.bible.com/116/hab.1.5.nlt

Habakkuk 1:12 NLT. Retrieved from https://www.bible.com/116/hab.1.12.nlt

Habakkuk 1:17 NLT. Retrieved from https://www.bible.com/116/hab.1.17.nlt

Habakkuk 2:3b NLT. Retrieved from https://www.bible.com/116/hab.2.3.nlt

1 Samuel 17:37 NLT. Retrieved from https://www.bible.com/116/1sa.17.37.nlt

Habakkuk 3:17-19 NLT. Retrieved from https://www.bible.com/116/hab.3.17-19.nlt

Jackson, Heather. (n.d.) Brave: Experiencing God in the waiting. Retrieved from https://www.bible.com/en/reading-plans/12328

Chapter 7

1 John 5:14-15 NLT. Retrieved from https://www.bible.com/116/1jn.5.14-15.nlt

Ephesians 3:20 NLT. Retrieved from https://www.bible.com/116/eph.3.20.nlt

Romans 8:28 NLT. Retrieved from https://www.bible.com/116/rom.8.28.nlt

Romans 8:37 NLT. Retrieved from https://www.bible.com/116/rom.8.37.nlt

1 Peter 5:7 NLT. Retrieved from https://www.bible.com/116/1pe.5.7.nlt

Matthew 6:25-33 NLT. Retrieved from https://www.bible.com/116/mat.6.25-33.nlt

Psalm 27:14 NLT. Retrieved from https://www.bible.com/116/psa.27.14.nlt

Psalm 5:3 NLT. Retrieved from https://www.bible.com/116/psa.5.3.nlt

Psalm 37:7 NLT. Retrieved from https://www.bible.com/116/psa.37.7.nlt

Psalm 40:1 NLT. Retrieved from https://www.bible.com/116/psa.40.1.nlt

Psalm 62:5 NLT. Retrieved from https://www.bible.com/116/psa.62.5.nlt

Isaiah 30:18 NLT. Retrieved from https://www.bible.com/116/isa.30.18.nlt

Lamentations 3:26 NLT. Retrieved from https://www.bible.com/116/lam.3.26.nlt

Daniel 12:12 NLT. Retrieved from https://www.bible.com/116/dan.12.12.nlt

Micah 7:7 NLT. Retrieved from https://www.bible.com/116/mic.7.7.nlt

Habakkuk 2:3 NLT. Retrieved from https://www.bible.com/116/hab.2.3.nlt

Romans 8:25 NLT. Retrieved from https://www.bible.com/116/rom.8.25.nlt

Romans 15:4 NLT. Retrieved from https://www.bible.com/116/rom.15.4.nlt

Hebrews 6:15 NLT. Retrieved from https://www.bible.com/116/heb.6.15.nlt

2 Peter 3:14 NLT. Retrieved from https://www.bible.com/116/2pe.3.14.nlt

Isaiah 40:31 NLT. Retrieved from https://www.bible.com/116/isa.40.31.nlt

Final Thoughts

Matthew 6:33 NIV. Retrieved from https://www.bible.com/111/mat.6.33.niv

Made in the USA
Coppell, TX
19 July 2020

31355335R00075